EXPLORE!

FORCE O

MW01043139

TSUNAMIS

BY MONIKA DAVIES

Please visit our website, www.enslow.com. For a free color catalog of all our high-quality books, call toll free 1-800-398-2504 or fax 1-877-980-4454.

Library of Congress Cataloging-in-Publication Data

Names: Davies, Monika, author.
Title: Tsunamis / Monika Davies.
Description: New York : Enslow Publishing, [2021] | Series: Force of nature
   | Includes index.
Identifiers: LCCN 2019057086 | ISBN 9781978518520 (library binding) | ISBN
   9781978518513 (paperback) | ISBN 9781978518537 (ebook)
Subjects: LCSH: Tsunamis–Juvenile literature.
Classification: LCC GC221.5 .D38 2021 | DDC 551.46/37–dc23
LC record available at https://lccn.loc.gov/2019057086

Published in 2021 by
Enslow Publishing
101 West 23rd Street, Suite #240
New York, NY 10011

Designer: Katelyn E. Reynolds
Editor: Monika Davies

Photo credits: Cover, p. 1 IgorZh/Shutterstock.com; cover, pp. 1–48 (series art) Merfin/Shutterstock.com; p. 5 mTaira/Shutterstock.com; p. 7 Tony Craddock/Shutterstock.com; p. 8 QAI Publishing/Universal Images Group via Getty Images; pp. 9, 27, 37 STR/AFP via Getty Images; p. 10 elgol/E+/Getty Images; p. 11 Sadatsugu Tomizawa/ AFP via Getty Images; pp. 12, 44 AFP/AFP via Getty Images; p. 13 Tim Graham/ The Image Bank/Getty Images Plus; p. 14 Kyodo News Stills via Getty Images; p. 15 Encyclopaedia Britannica/UIG Via Getty Images; p. 17 Chris + Mayet Palacio/Moment/Getty Images Plus; p. 18 Jiji Press/AFP via Getty Images; p. 19 Doroniuk Anastasiia/ Shutterstock.com; p. 20 Bill Brennan/Perspectives/Getty Images Plus; p. 21 Hariandi Hafid/SOPA Images/ LightRocket via Getty Images; p. 22 Medesulda/DigitalVision Vectors/Getty Images; p. 23 Tomas Nevesely/ Shutterstock.com; p. 24 MoreISO/iStock/Getty Images Plus; p. 25 Noel Celis/AFP via Getty Images; p. 28 Sena Vidanagama/AFP via Getty Images; p. 29 Photography by Mangiwau/Moment/Getty Images; p. 30 Dimas Ardian/ Getty Images; p. 31 Ævar Arnfjörð Bjarmason/Wikipedia.org; p. 32 Choo Youn-Kong/AFP via Getty Images; p. 33 Eko Siswono Toyudho/Anadolu Agency/Getty Images; p. 34 Petr Dlouhý/Wikipedia.org; p. 35 DigitalGlobe via Getty Images; p. 38 Pacific Marine Environmental Laboratory/Wikipedia.org; p. 39 NOAA/Wikipedia.org; pp. 40, 41 Marco Garcia/Getty Images; p. 42 Kyodo News Stills via Getty Images; p. 43 The Asahi Shimbun via Getty Images; p. 45 Patrick M. Bonafede/U.S. Navy via Getty Images.

Printed in the United States of America

Some of the images in this book illustrate individuals who are models. The depictions do not imply actual situations or events.

CPSIA compliance information: Batch #BS20ENS: For further information contact Enslow Publishing, New York, New York, at 1-800-542-2595.

Find us on

CONTENTS

 Tsunami Terror...4

 Wicked Waves 6

 Tsunami Beginnings............................16

 Historic Tsunamis 26

 Preparing for the Future 36

 Glossary 46

 For More Information 47

 Index..48

WORDS IN THE GLOSSARY APPEAR IN **BOLD** TYPE
THE FIRST TIME THEY ARE USED IN THE TEXT.

TSUNAMI TERROR

Tsunamis are easily one of the deadliest and most **destructive** forces of nature. These series of huge, powerful waves of water have been responsible for countless deaths and billions of dollars of property **damage**. This force of nature can drown an entire city in water.

Every year, there are usually two tsunamis that cause destruction near their starting point. Every 10 years, there are approximately two tsunamis that cause destruction as far away as 620 miles (1,000 km) from their starting point. In this book, we'll look at how a tsunami develops, which historic tsunamis left **devastating** aftermaths, and how people can recognize the signs of an approaching tsunami.

THE INCREDIBLE POWER OF A TSUNAMI CAN DESTROY ALMOST ANYTHING IN ITS PATH. CARS AND TRUCKS, BUILDINGS, AND EVEN STONE STRUCTURES ARE NO MATCH FOR A TSUNAMI.

WICKED WAVES

The term "tsunami" comes from the Japanese words *tsu* (harbor) and *nami* (wave). A tsunami is actually a series of powerful waves that travel great distances across the world's oceans very quickly. A tsunami wave can be 60 miles (97 km) long and 100 feet (30 m) tall.

Most waves are created by wind blowing across the surface of the water. The size and strength of these waves depend on the speed of the wind. Tsunamis, however, are created when a sudden disturbance—such as an earthquake, volcano, or **landslide**—moves a large amount of water.

6

EARTHQUAKE:

A SHAKING OF THE GROUND CAUSED BY THE MOVEMENT OF EARTH'S CRUST

TSUNAMI HAZARD ZONE

IN CASE OF EARTHQUAKE GO TO HIGH GROUND OR INLAND

PLACES THAT ARE MORE LIKELY TO HAVE TSUNAMIS MAY HAVE SIGNS LIKE THIS ONE POSTED TO REMIND PEOPLE HOW TO STAY SAFE.

The size and strength of a tsunami's waves depend on the power of the event that created them. Strong earthquakes and large landslides release great energy that can move, or displace, a lot of water. While the force of the energy pushes the water up, gravity pulls it down. This causes waves to spread in all directions.

"RING OF FIRE"

PACIFIC OCEAN

MOST TSUNAMIS OCCUR IN THE PACIFIC OCEAN. TSUNAMIS OFTEN ORIGINATE IN THE "RING OF FIRE," AN AREA WHERE UNDERWATER VOLCANOES AND EARTHQUAKES ARE COMMON. THE RING OF FIRE RUNS ALONG THE BOUNDARIES BETWEEN **TECTONIC PLATES**.

SINCE TSUNAMI WAVES CAN BE TALL, THEY MAY AFFECT INLAND AREAS THAT ARE UP TO 50 FEET (15 M) ABOVE SEA LEVEL.

EXPLORE MORE

WHILE 80 PERCENT OF TSUNAMIS BEGIN IN THE "RING OF FIRE," THEY HAVE ALSO FORMED IN OTHER BODIES OF WATER, INCLUDING THE CARIBBEAN AND MEDITERRANEAN SEAS AND THE INDIAN AND ATLANTIC OCEANS.

Tsunamis have long wavelengths. A tsunami's wavelength may be from 60 miles (97 km) to 120 miles (193 km). It may take more than an hour after the first crest reaches land for the second crest to arrive.

In the deep ocean, tsunami waves barely rise above the ocean's surface. This makes it difficult to spot tsunamis from the air or even in a boat on the water. It's usually only when the tsunami reaches the shoreline that it can be identified easily.

WAVELENGTH:
THE DISTANCE FROM THE TOP, OR CREST, OF ONE WAVE TO THE TOP OF THE NEXT WAVE

WAVES CREATED BY WIND CAN BE VERY POWERFUL, BUT THEY AREN'T NEARLY AS LONG, POWERFUL, OR FAST AS TSUNAMI WAVES. WAVES CREATED BY THE WIND USUALLY TRAVEL AT SPEEDS BETWEEN 5 AND 60 MILES (8 AND 97 KM) PER HOUR.

JET SPEED

While wind-driven waves move in the same direction as the wind, tsunami waves move much like the ripples created by tossing a pebble into a pond. Tsunamis can travel through an ocean at speeds of up to 500 miles (800 km) per hour. Some tsunamis are even faster. At such high speeds, a tsunami can cross an ocean in just a few hours. Tsunamis don't lose much energy as they travel through deep water. The energy moves through the water rather than on top as with wind-driven waves. The deeper the water, the faster the tsunami moves.

A TSUNAMI WAVE CAN TRAVEL AT THE SAME SPEED AS A JET PLANE! THIS MAKES TSUNAMIS A SWIFT FORCE OF NATURE.

 A TSUNAMI IS SUCH A DESTRUCTIVE FORCE OF NATURE THAT IT CAN CLEAR AN ENTIRE BEACH! IF YOU HEAR A TSUNAMI WARNING, STAY AWAY FROM ANY NEARBY BEACHES.

EXPLORE
MORE

SOMETIMES, TSUNAMIS
ARE MISTAKENLY
CALLED TIDAL WAVES.
REAL TIDAL WAVES
AREN'T AS VIOLENT OR
LARGE. IN FACT, A TIDAL
WAVE IS ANOTHER NAME
FOR THE TIDE.
THIS TWICE-DAILY
OCCURRENCE IS
CAUSED BY THE
GRAVITY OF THE MOON
AND THE SUN PULLING
ON A BODY OF WATER,
CAUSING IT TO RISE
AND FALL.

AT HIGH TIDE, THE WATER WILL COME MUCH
HIGHER ONTO THE SHORE THAN AT LOW TIDE.

As a tsunami races toward shallow coastal waters, it begins to slow down. A tsunami that was once traveling at 500 miles (800 km) per hour through the deep ocean may slow to 30 miles (48 km) per hour. This sudden change in speed causes tsunami waters to "pile up" and reach up to 100 feet (30 m) above sea level.

THIS PHOTOGRAPH OF A TSUNAMI HITTING JAPAN CLEARLY SHOWS WATER RISING ABOVE HOMES AND OTHER BUILDINGS.

TSUNAMI TIMELINE

A tsunami has a point of generation, or a starting point from where tsunami waves extend out. From generation, the tsunami waves propagate, or travel, through the open ocean. While tsunami waves have long wavelengths, the height of the waves isn't high. Wave height is measured from the crest to the trough, or the highest point to the lowest point of the wave. In open waters, a tsunami wave may measure only about 1 to 2 feet (30 to 60 cm) high. However, when the waves draw close to the shore, the waves will crest, or rise up, to enormous heights.

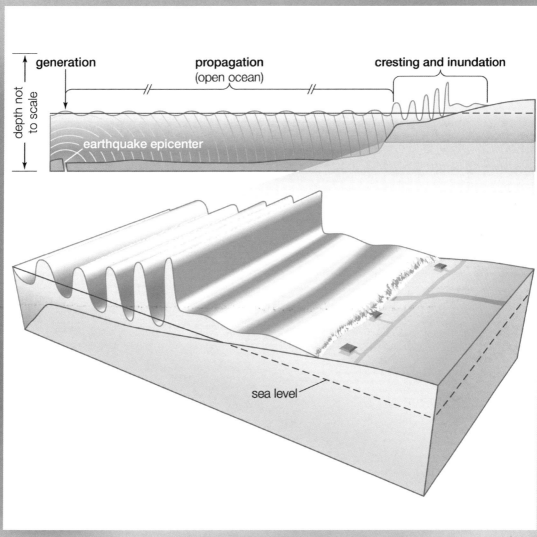

AN EARTHQUAKE CAN CAUSE A TSUNAMI. THE EARTHQUAKE'S **EPICENTER** MARKS THE POINT OF GENERATION. WHEN TSUNAMI WAVES INUNDATE AN AREA, THIS MEANS THE AREA IS COVERED WITH A FLOOD OF WATER.

TSUNAMI BEGINNINGS

Tsunamis are often the result of large underwater earthquakes. Earth's outer layer, or crust, is composed of huge sections called plates on which the continents and ocean floor rest. These plates move very slowly on a layer of hot, soft rock. When plates meet, pressure builds up between them until they suddenly snap out of place. They may slide past each other, crumble, or slide over or under each other.

The energy released by this sharp movement causes the ground to shake and the water around it to move. Fortunately, most earthquakes don't generate enough force to create a tsunami.

THE U.S. GEOLOGICAL SURVEY (USGS) **ESTIMATES** THAT THERE ARE 500,000 **DETECTABLE** EARTHQUAKES EVERY YEAR. PEOPLE FEEL THE EFFECTS OF 100,000 OF THESE EARTHQUAKES, WHILE ONLY 100 WILL CAUSE ACTUAL DAMAGE.

EXPLORE MORE

THE MOMENT MAGNITUDE SCALE MEASURES THE MAGNITUDE OF EARTHQUAKES. THE SCALE RANGES FROM 1 TO 10, WITH 1 AS THE WEAKEST QUAKE. GENERALLY, DEADLY TSUNAMIS ARE CAUSED BY EARTHQUAKES THAT ARE MAGNITUDE 7.6 OR HIGHER.

MAGNITUDE:
A MEASURE OF THE POWER OF AN EARTHQUAKE

When a tsunami reaches land, it causes the most damage to areas within 1 mile (1.6 km) of the shoreline. Sometimes, a tsunami crashes onto shore with a tall, violent wave called a bore. Most often, it looks as if the ocean tide is rising up quickly, or surging, onto the shore.

MIYAKO, JAPAN
2011

18

OTHER CAUSES

Volcanoes, landslides, and meteorites are three more causes of tsunamis. When one of Earth's plates slides under another, the sinking plate carries water that lowers the melting point of rock and allows **magma** to form. Two plates pulling apart can also allow magma to rise to Earth's surface. When magma escapes through a volcanic eruption, the explosion can cause a tsunami. Underwater landslides can cause tsunamis too. But, since earthquakes **trigger** some underwater landslides, earthquakes are sometimes considered the true cause. There are no known meteorite-caused tsunamis in history. However, scientists think a large meteorite crashed into Earth over 3 billion years ago and created a powerful tsunami that swept over the entire planet—several times!

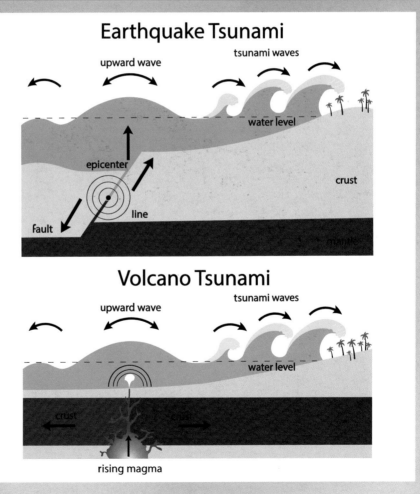

WHEN AN EARTHQUAKE STRIKES OR A VOLCANO ERUPTS UNDER THE SEA, THIS CAN CAUSE GIANT TSUNAMI WAVES TO DESTROY CITIES AND TOWNS, KNOCK DOWN STRUCTURES, AND DROWN PEOPLE.

Without tall waves, the water surface may appear calm, but underneath it's a different story. Powerful, churning water can easily pull people under, cause cars to float like toys, and rip buildings from the ground. Entire beaches can be washed away by a tsunami.

ONE OF THE MOST DEVASTATING TSUNAMIS IN RECENT HISTORY WAS THE 2004 INDIAN OCEAN TSUNAMI. IT FLOODED VILLAGES AND CITIES, CAUSING MASS DESTRUCTION.

CHURNING:
STIRRING OR SHAKING FORCEFULLY

THIS PHOTOGRAPH SHOWS THE AFTERMATH OF AN EARTHQUAKE AND TSUNAMI THAT HIT SULAWESI, AN INDONESIAN ISLAND IN SOUTHEAST ASIA, ON SEPTEMBER 28, 2018. A DESTRUCTIVE EARTHQUAKE FIRST STRUCK SULAWESI, LATER FOLLOWED BY TSUNAMI WAVES 20 FEET (6 M) HIGH.

A person on the beach may notice that water on the shoreline moves back and forth. Just before a wave hits the shore, the water drains back into the ocean or lake. The same thing often happens just before a tsunami reaches shore, only on a much bigger scale.

Many times, water along the coastline will completely drain away when a tsunami approaches. This is because the low point of the wave, called the trough, often reaches shore first. When it does, it causes water along the coast to pull back toward the sea, exposing large amounts of seafloor. This vacuum effect warns that the wave's crest will soon follow.

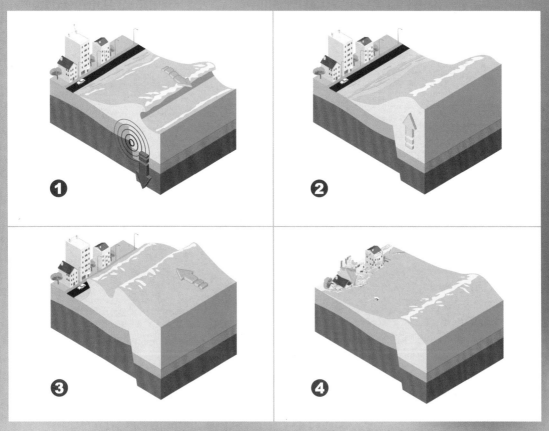

THIS ILLUSTRATION SHOWS HOW A DEADLY TSUNAMI DEVELOPS AND FINALLY CRASHES INTO A SHORELINE.

EVACUATE:
TO WITHDRAW FROM A PLACE FOR PROTECTION

EXPLORE MORE

JUST AS WAVES MAKE A CRASHING SOUND, A TSUNAMI'S INCREDIBLE POWER IS EXTREMELY LOUD. SOME PEOPLE HAVE COMPARED THE SOUND TO TRAINS OR JET ENGINES. WHEN PEOPLE HEAR THE NOISE, THEY SHOULD EVACUATE TO HIGH GROUND AS QUICKLY AS POSSIBLE.

AS SOON AS YOU OR A FAMILY MEMBER HEARS AN OFFICIAL TSUNAMI WARNING OR SEES A SIGN OF A TSUNAMI'S APPROACH, IT'S IMPORTANT TO IMMEDIATELY EVACUATE THE AREA. DON'T WAIT!

NATURE'S WARNING SIGNS

Officials will often release warnings of a tsunami through television, radio, or text broadcasts. However, it's also important to know nature's warning signs that a tsunami is approaching. If you're standing near water and notice a large area of seafloor is suddenly visible, this is a clear sign that a tsunami is on its way. If you're near water and experience a strong shaking of the ground from an earthquake, killer tsunami waves may be on their way. Some people also report hearing a loud "roar" when a tsunami is en route. All of these warning signs let you know it's time to immediately leave the area.

IT TAKES ABOUT 5 MINUTES FOR THE FIRST CREST OF A TSUNAMI TO REACH SHORE AFTER THE TROUGH DRAINS THE COAST. THIS SHOULD ALERT PEOPLE ALONG THE COASTLINE. OTHER WAVES CAN FOLLOW ANYWHERE FROM 5 TO 90 MINUTES AFTER THE FIRST WAVE HITS.

24

IN 2010, AN EARTHQUAKE IN CHILE HAD SCIENTISTS AS FAR AWAY AS THE PHILIPPINES WORKING ON MODELS LIKE THIS ONE TO PREDICT, OR USE KNOWLEDGE TO GUESS, IF A TSUNAMI WOULD HIT THEM.

25

HISTORIC TSUNAMIS

On December 26, 2004, the most powerful earthquake in 40 years shook the seafloor beneath the Indian Ocean. Measuring 9.1 on the moment magnitude scale, this massive quake sent a series of killer waves speeding in all directions across the Indian Ocean. In just a few hours, tsunami waves crashed onto the shores of 13 countries around the Indian Ocean, killing more than 200,000 people.

The tsunami was so powerful that its destructive waves traveled more than 3,000 miles (4,800 km), causing damage along the east coast of Africa. In some areas, the earthquake created tsunami waves that reached 50 feet (15 m) tall.

THIS PHOTOGRAPH SHOWS THE SEVERE FLOODING AND DESTRUCTION OF A BEACH IN SOUTHERN INDIA FOLLOWING THE 2004 INDIAN OCEAN TSUNAMI.

THE COUNTRIES THAT SUFFERED A CONSIDERABLE AMOUNT OF DAMAGE FROM THE INDIAN OCEAN TSUNAMI WERE INDONESIA, SRI LANKA, INDIA, THE MALDIVES, AND THAILAND. THIS 2004 PHOTOGRAPH SHOWS THE TSUNAMI'S DESTRUCTION ALONG THE COASTLINE OF SRI LANKA.

EXPLORE MORE

THE INDIAN OCEAN EARTHQUAKE WAS CAUSED BY TWO PLATES THAT HAD PRESSED AGAINST EACH OTHER FOR HUNDREDS OF YEARS. WHEN THEY SUDDENLY SNAPPED OUT OF PLACE, THEY RELEASED ENERGY THAT SCIENTISTS ESTIMATE WAS EQUAL TO 23,000 **ATOMIC BOMBS**.

COASTLINE:

THE AREA OR LAND ALONG THE EDGE OF A SEA OR OCEAN

THIS PHOTOGRAPH SHOWS THE POOR CONDITION OF THE COAST OF INDONESIA EIGHT MONTHS AFTER THE TSUNAMI HIT. RECOVERY FROM TSUNAMIS CAN TAKE YEARS.

Unfortunately, many people affected by the Indian Ocean tsunami didn't recognize one of the warning signs. Just before the tsunami reached land, several coastlines were drained of water, **stranding** boats and fish. Because this was such a rare sight, many curious people wandered onto the bare seafloor. A few minutes later, the tsunami waves rushed onto the shoreline, swallowing everything in their path.

MEULABOH, INDONESIA

LIFESAVING KNOWLEDGE

A man in India saved many people in his village when he remembered what he had learned about tsunamis from a television documentary, or a program that discusses facts about real people and events. He knew an exposed seafloor was a warning sign of a tsunami and warned his community. He then helped lead his neighbors to higher ground far from the ocean. A British newspaper told the story of a young girl on vacation in Thailand who saved her family when she recalled what she had learned about tsunamis in her **geography** class.

THIS MAP SHOWS THE STARTING POINT OF THE 2004 INDIAN OCEAN TSUNAMI, AS WELL AS WHICH COUNTRIES WERE AFFECTED BY THIS MASSIVE NATURAL DISASTER.

The Indian Ocean tsunami destroyed thousands of miles of coastline and flooded entire islands. By the time the water level returned to normal, hundreds of thousands of people were dead or missing, and millions more were homeless.

FLOOD:
A LARGE STREAM OF RUSHING WATER THAT COVERS LAND THAT'S NORMALLY DRY

MANY ANIMALS SENSED THE DANGER OF THE 2004 INDIAN OCEAN TSUNAMI. PEOPLE REPORTED SEEING MULTIPLE ANIMALS RUN TO HIGHER GROUND JUST BEFORE THE TSUNAMI ARRIVED.

2018 INDONESIA TSUNAMIS

In 2018, the country of Indonesia suffered severe damage from two massive tsunamis caused by different events. On September 28, a major earthquake struck Sulawesi, an Indonesian island. Although earthquakes can sometimes result in a tsunami, the powerful waves that hit Palu shortly afterward weren't expected by residents. The waves measured up to 18 feet (5 m) tall. Over 2,000 people died in the double disasters. On December 22, a tsunami hit the islands of Java and Sumatra, leaving over 400 dead. It's believed undersea landslides triggered by a volcanic eruption caused the second tsunami.

THIS PHOTOGRAPH SHOWS THE DECEMBER 2018 TSUNAMI'S CONSIDERABLE DAMAGE TO THE BANTEN PROVINCE ON THE ISLAND OF JAVA. THE TSUNAMI'S DEADLY AND POWERFUL WAVES CAME WITHOUT WARNING.

33

On March 11, 2011, a massive earthquake struck off the coast of Japan's main island, Honshu. This quake measured 9.1 on the moment magnitude scale. The tsunami it created devastated parts of Japan and also caused destruction in other countries in the Pacific Ocean. Giant waves flooded cities and villages, swept away cars and trucks, and destroyed homes and businesses. Even the West Coast of the United States suffered damage from the tsunami.

Japan has suffered many earthquakes throughout its history. The 2011 earthquake, however, was the strongest to ever strike the country. Yet the earthquake caused only a small fraction of the damage, thanks to earthquake-ready buildings. Most of the damage was caused by the tsunami.

TSUNAMI DANGER ZONES

■ HIGH RISK
■ MEDIUM RISK
□ LOW RISK

ATLANTIC OCEAN

PACIFIC OCEAN

INDIAN OCEAN

PACIFIC OCEAN

THIS MAP SHOWS THE LEVEL OF RISK OF A TSUNAMI STRIKING DIFFERENT PARTS OF THE WORLD.

RADIOACTIVE:
PUTTING OUT HARMFUL ENERGY IN THE FORM OF TINY PARTICLES

EXPLORE MORE

ON AUGUST 26, 1883, ONE OF THE LARGEST AND MOST DESTRUCTIVE TSUNAMIS EVER RECORDED OCCURRED. THE INDONESIAN VOLCANO KRAKATOA, OR KRAKATAU, EXPLODED, CREATING TSUNAMI WAVES THAT REACHED 120 FEET (37 M) HIGH. MANY TOWNS AND VILLAGES ON NEARBY ISLANDS WERE DESTROYED, AND ABOUT 36,000 PEOPLE WERE KILLED.

WHEN TSUNAMI WATERS FLOODED THE FUKUSHIMA DAIICHI NUCLEAR POWER PLANT, DEADLY RADIOACTIVITY WAS RELEASED INTO THE WATER AND AIR.

PREPARING FOR THE FUTURE

There's currently no way to predict when a tsunami will occur. The earthquakes, landslides, and volcanic eruptions that cause tsunamis also cannot be predicted and these don't always result in a tsunami anyway. In addition, once a tsunami begins, it's only a matter of minutes or hours before it reaches land. For these reasons, it's hard to keep those in areas tsunamis are most likely safe from these terrifying forces of nature.

PREDICT:
TO GUESS WHAT WILL HAPPEN IN THE FUTURE BASED ON FACTS OR KNOWLEDGE

TSUNAMIS CAN TRAVEL UP RIVERS AND STREAMS THAT LEAD TO THE OCEAN. TSUNAMI WAVES CAN ALSO BOUNCE REPEATEDLY OFF THE EDGES OF BAYS AND HARBORS, CAUSING THE WAVES TO GROW LARGER.

EXPLORE MORE

THE COAST OF THE NORTHWESTERN UNITED STATES AND SOUTHWESTERN CANADA IS LOCATED NEAR TWO PLATES CAPABLE OF CREATING POWERFUL EARTHQUAKES. IT HAS BEEN ROUGHLY 300 YEARS SINCE AN EARTHQUAKE SIMILAR TO THE ONE THAT STRUCK JAPAN IN 2011 HAS OCCURRED THERE. AN EARTHQUAKE OF THAT SIZE COULD CREATE A DEADLY TSUNAMI.

However, scientists have placed sensors on the ocean floor to detect activity. Once movement occurs, they use computers to create models that predict wave size and the time of their arrival on land. Scientists also use sea-level gauges to help identify tsunamis. Tsunami warning centers use all this information to provide warnings to the public.

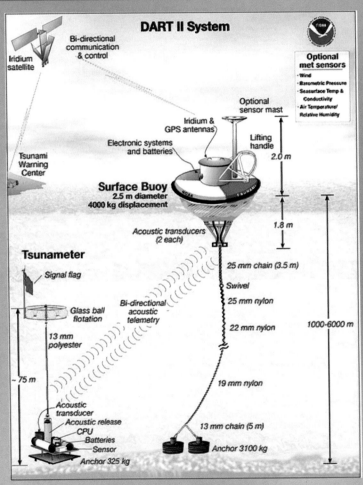

THE U.S. NATIONAL OCEANIC AND ATMOSPHERIC ADMINISTRATION (NOAA) HAS PUT IN DART STATIONS AROUND THE OCEAN IN AREAS WHERE TSUNAMIS HAVE BEEN COMMON IN THE PAST. DART STANDS FOR DEEP-OCEAN ASSESSMENT AND REPORTING OF TSUNAMIS.

EXPLORE MORE

A GAUGE IS A TOOL THAT MEASURES THE AMOUNT OF SOMETHING. TIDE GAUGES MEASURE THE HEIGHT OF THE SEA LEVEL, AS WELL AS TIDE LEVELS. BY TRACKING AND MONITORING THE HEIGHT OF SEA AND TIDE LEVELS, SCIENTISTS CAN TRACK WHEN EITHER LEVEL EXPERIENCES A SIGNIFICANT INCREASE.

SENSOR:
A TOOL THAT CAN DETECT CHANGES IN ITS SURROUNDINGS

DART STATIONS CONSIST OF A SEAFLOOR BOTTOM PRESSURE RECORDER ATTACHED TO A FLOATING DEVICE ALSO KNOWN AS A SURFACE BUOY (SHOWN HERE) THAT SENDS DATA BACK TO THE NOAA.

The best way to protect yourself against a tsunami is to act quickly after receiving a warning. If you live in an area that may be affected by a tsunami, be sure to get to higher ground as soon as you hear a tsunami warning, feel an earthquake, or see the coastal waters draw back.

WHEN MAJOR EARTHQUAKES HAPPEN IN THE OCEAN, SCIENTISTS MONITOR CONDITIONS TO SEE IF A TSUNAMI WILL OCCUR.

U.S. TSUNAMI WARNING CENTERS

The United States has two tsunami warning centers, both of which are open and run by staff members 24 hours a day, 7 days a week. The National Tsunami Warning Center is based in Palmer, Alaska, while the Pacific Tsunami Warning Center is found near Honolulu, Hawaii. Each center is in charge of monitoring water levels in different ocean areas, earthquakes across the globe, and other data points. The Pacific Tsunami Warning Center is the main international forecast center for potential tsunamis in the Pacific and Caribbean basins, or bodies of water.

SINCE THE PACIFIC TSUNAMI WARNING CENTER MONITORS THE PACIFIC BASIN, IT IS IN CHARGE OF SENDING SEVERE TSUNAMI WARNINGS TO NEARLY EVERY COUNTRY THAT BORDERS THE PACIFIC BASIN, AS WELL AS MANY PACIFIC ISLANDS.

It's also important to remember that a tsunami is a series of waves. The waves that follow the first can be even larger, and surging waters are equally dangerous. When it comes to tsunamis, every minute counts.

Floodwaters caused by tsunamis can contain harmful chemicals and waste. Avoid eating food or drinking water that has come into contact with floodwater. People should follow the orders of officials before, during, and after a tsunami.

A TSUNAMI'S SERIES OF WAVES IS ALSO KNOWN AS A TSUNAMI WAVE TRAIN. DUE TO THIS SERIES OF WAVES, THE DANGER FROM A TSUNAMI CAN LAST FOR HOURS.

AFTER IT BEGINS, A LARGE TSUNAMI CAN CONTINUE THROUGH BODIES OF
WATER FOR A FEW DAYS.

From 1900 to 2015, tsunamis started in multiple bodies of water, but the majority—around 78 percent—happened in the Pacific Ocean. In comparison, around 8 percent of tsunamis occurred in the Atlantic Ocean and Caribbean Sea, 6 percent in the Mediterranean Sea, 5 percent in the Indian Ocean, and the remainder in other bodies of water.

However, devastating and far-reaching tsunamis usually happen only twice every 10 years. While they're more rare than other natural disasters, tsunamis are still a destructive force of nature. Knowing a tsunami's warning signs can keep you and your family safe if one strikes nearby.

THE EFFECT OF CLIMATE CHANGE

Climate change has led to ocean surface temperatures increasing, as well as higher sea levels. Earth's glaciers are also melting as global temperatures rise. Some of these melting glaciers used to hold up parts of mountainsides. When they melt, these glaciers may trigger large landslides that lead to tsunamis. There's now evidence that these landslide-triggered tsunamis may become more frequent in the future. Higher sea levels will also likely lead to taller tsunami waves that reach further inland. This would heighten the impact and devastation of a tsunami.

CLIMATE CHANGE:
LONG-TERM CHANGE IN EARTH'S CLIMATE, CAUSED PARTLY BY HUMAN ACTIVITIES SUCH AS BURNING OIL AND NATURAL GAS

SINCE 1900, THE MAJORITY OF TSUNAMIS HAVE STARTED OFF THE SHORES OF JAPAN, RUSSIA, AND INDONESIA.

GLOSSARY

atomic bomb A bomb whose explosive power comes from energy released by splitting atoms.

damage Harm; also, to cause harm.

destructive Causing damage or ruin.

detectable Able to be noticed or discovered.

devastating Causing widespread damage.

epicenter The specific place on Earth's surface right above where an earthquake starts.

estimate To make a careful guess about an answer based on the known facts.

geography The study of Earth and its features.

landslide The sudden movement of rocks and dirt down a hill or mountain.

magma Hot, liquid rock inside Earth.

strand To cause something or someone to be left behind.

tectonic plate One of the moveable masses of rock that create Earth's surface.

trigger To cause something to begin or happen.

FOR MORE INFORMATION

BOOKS

Larson, Kirsten. *Tsunamis*. Vero Beach, FL: Rourke Educational Media, 2015.

Squire, Ann O. *Tsunamis*. New York, NY: Children's Press, 2016.

Tarshis, Lauren. *I Survived the Japanese Tsunami, 2011*. New York, NY: Scholastic Press, 2013.

WEBSITES

Tsunamis
www.bbc.co.uk/bitesize/guides/zbfrd2p/revision/1
Find out more about the impacts of tsunamis at this site.

Tsunamis
www.ready.gov/tsunamis
Discover how you can stay safe before, during, and after a tsunami.

What Is a Tsunami?
spaceplace.nasa.gov/tsunami/en/
Learn more about tsunamis here.

INDEX

B

bore, 18

C

climate change, 45

D

damage/destruction, 4, 18, 20, 26, 30, 32, 33, 34, 35

deaths, 4, 26, 32, 33, 35

E

earthquakes, 6, 8, 16, 17, 19, 24, 26, 28, 33, 34, 36, 37, 40, 41

H

height, 6, 14, 15, 26, 33, 35

I

Indian Ocean tsunami (2004), 26, 28, 30, 31, 32

Indonesia tsunami (1883), 35

Indonesia tsunamis (2018), 33

J

Japan tsunami (2011), 34, 37

L

landslides, 6, 8, 19, 33, 36, 45

M

meteorites, 19

moment magnitude scale, 17, 26, 34

S

sound/noise, 23, 24

speed, 11, 14

T

tidal waves, 13

V

volcanoes, 6, 19, 33, 35, 36

W

warning centers, 38, 41

warning signs, 22, 23, 24, 30, 31, 40, 44

wavelengths, 10, 15

wind-driven waves, 6, 11